A Walk in the Mountains

by Kim Borland

PEARSON

Scott
Foresman

Editorial Offices: Glenview, Illinois • Parsippany, New Jersey • New York, New York
Sales Offices: Needham, Massachusetts • Duluth, Georgia • Glenview, Illinois
Coppell, Texas • Ontario, California • Mesa, Arizona

Every effort has been made to secure permission and provide appropriate credit for photographic material. The publisher deeply regrets any omission and pledges to correct errors called to its attention in subsequent editions.

Unless otherwise acknowledged, all photographs are the property of Scott Foresman, a division of Pearson Education.

Photo locators denoted as follows: Top (T), Center (C), Bottom (B), Left (L), Right (R), Background (Bkgd)

1 © Galen Rowell/Corbis; 4 © Jay Dickman/Corbis; 5 © Paul A. Souders/Corbis; 6 (L) © Galen Rowell/Corbis, 6 (R) © M.D./Corbis; 7 (C) © Pat Jerrold; Papilio/Corbis, 7 (Bkgrd) © Ric Ergenbright/Corbis; 8 (L) © Ron Sanford/Corbis, 8 (R) © Tom Brakefield/ Corbis, 9 (R) © Steve Austin; Papilio/Corbis, 9 (L) © Kennan Ward/Corbis; 11a Otter Niall Benvie/Corbis, 12 © Robert Landau/Corbis

ISBN: 0-328-13242-3

6 7 8 9 10 V010 14 13 12 11 10 09 08 07

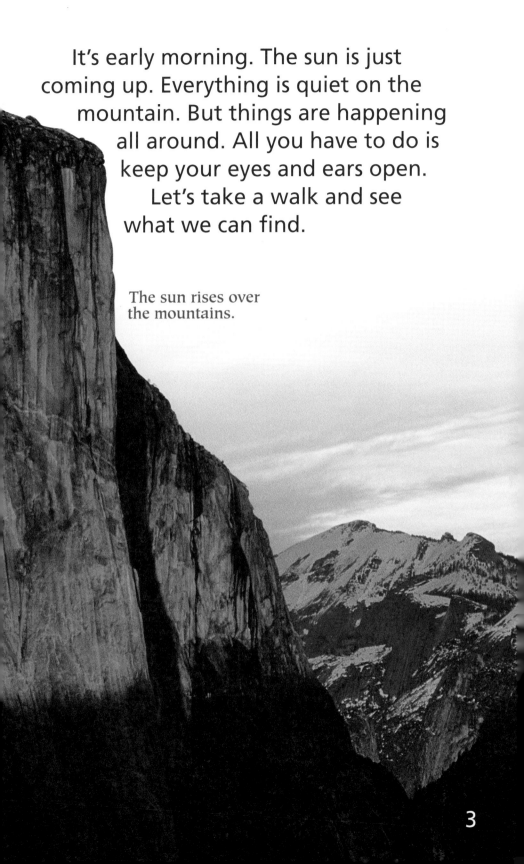

It's early morning. The sun is just coming up. Everything is quiet on the mountain. But things are happening all around. All you have to do is keep your eyes and ears open. Let's take a walk and see what we can find.

The sun rises over the mountains.

Look up! Can you see the tops of the mountains? Some are sharp. Others are low and rounded.

These mountains are many, many years old.

The Appalachian Mountains are the oldest mountains in North America.

Some mountains are so tall that their tops are covered in snow. It is very cold at the top. The place where the snow begins is called the *snow line*. Can you see the snow line on this mountain?

The highest peak in North America is Mount McKinley in Alaska.

Mountains are home to all kinds of plants and animals. Not many things live near the top. It is too cold. But it is warmer on the lower part of the mountain. There are many plants and animals.

Mountain goats are good climbers. They can jump from rock to rock on mountain slopes.

Grizzly bears can be found in the Rocky Mountains.

Trees, flowers, and other plants grow on the grassy hills. Insects live here too. Bees buzz all around. Butterflies fly from flower to flower.

Edelweiss is a type of mountain flower. It has hairy leaves. They help it hold water.

Edelweiss is a flower found in Europe, Asia, and South America.

Forests grow on the lower parts of mountains.

The porcupine lives in these mountains all year long. It eats plants, twigs, and tree bark.

The golden eagle lives here too. It builds its nest way up high. But it flies down low to catch its food.

A golden eagle can glide for a long time without flapping its wings.

The porcupine has long sharp quills all over its body. They protect it from other animals.

Did you see that? A hare just hopped across our path. Its fur is brown. But it will turn snow white when winter comes.

Hares feed on the leaves and grass that they find in the forests.

A hare's white coat protects it from other animals.

This hare is starting to turn white for winter.

Look at this waterfall! The cold, clear water falls into a running stream below. The rushing water of a waterfall helps change the shape of a mountain. It slowly wears away the rock.

Yosemite National Park in California has the tallest waterfall in the United States.

All kinds of animals live in and around a mountain stream. Otters catch fish here. Deer and raccoons come for a drink.

Plants live near streams too. Their roots can find all the water they need.

Otters have webbed feet and are fast swimmers.

Raccoons are good climbers. They sometimes nest or hide in trees.

We've had a full day of exploring. But there is more to see and learn about this special place. So the next time you see a mountain, think about all the interesting plants and animals that live there—from the bottom to the very top!